Scottish Churches

by M. Muir

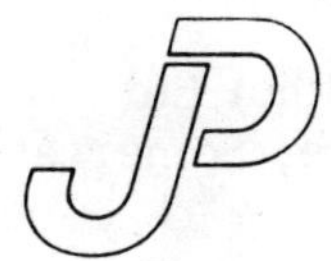

JAMES PIKE LTD
St Ives, Cornwall, England

Cover picture - Daviot Church, near Old Meldrum,
- Scottish Tourist Board.

First Edition 1975
ISBN 0 85932 098·7

Printed by: H S (Litho) Ltd
Weston-Super-Mare, Somerset

Kelso

Thirteen monks of the Benedictine Order from Tiron in France came to Scotland in 1113 at the invitation of David, Earl of Huntington, later the saintly David 1, son of Malcolm Canmore and his devout Queen Margaret. The original site offered near the Earl's castle in Selkirk proved unsuitable for the establishment of a monastery so in 1128 the foundations were laid in Kelso, of what was to become the richest and most powerful of the Border Abbeys. By 1165 Kelso Abbey was so important the privilege of wearing the mitre was granted to the Abbot by the Pope, thus giving him precedence over other abbots in Scotland. This distinction was enjoyed by his successors until 1420 when James I transferred the honour to the Prior of St. Andrews.

The position of the monastic settlement, so near the Border, meant that it was ravaged by fire, and plundered time and again during the wars with England. By 1560 the few monks still remaining abandoned the monastery and found refuge in neighbouring religious houses. After the Reformation the remains of the Abbey were sufficiently restored to allow it to become the Parish church of Kelso. So it remained until 1771 when deterioration of the fabric led to its closure as a place of worship.

The Abbey built in Norman style consisted of a chancel with north and south aisles, transept and nave without aisles. The two divisions of the transept form, with the nave, three arms of equal length enclosing the crossing above which rose a massive square tower. Of what still remains the most interesting parts are the south transept and the west front. The transept windows are bold and simple in construction and between the buttressed towers of the west front, is an arcaded gallery open to both nave and outside of the church. The rounded Norman arch of the recessed doorway has finely carved mouldings and capitals. Even today the sturdy ruins of this once famous Abbey still dominate the attractive county town of Kelso.

Dryburgh

Ten miles from Jedburgh on the north bank of the Tweed, in beautiful surroundings stands Dryburgh Abbey, where in the solitude of the Lady Aisle of the north transept lie the remains of Sir Walter Scott and Earl Haig. Only fragments remain of the Abbey founded in 1150 by Hugh de

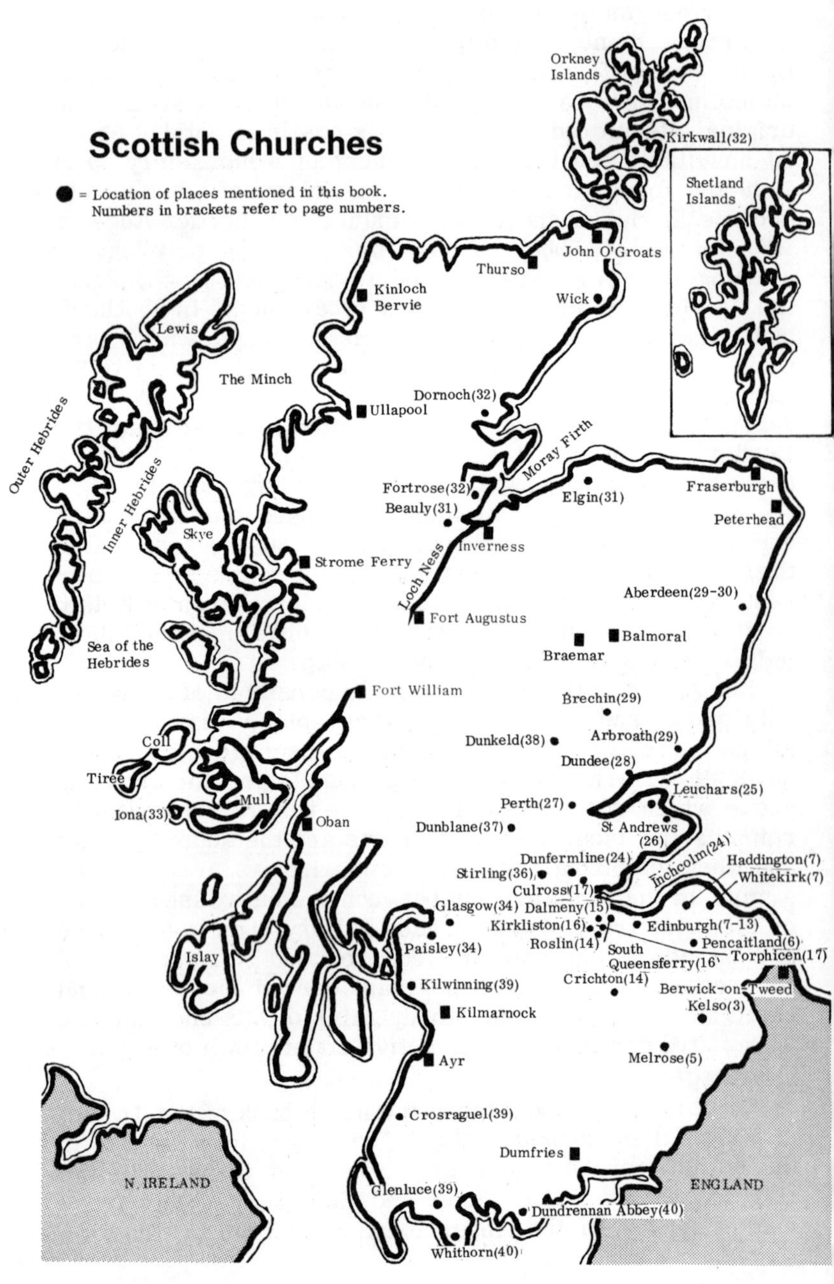

Scottish Churches
= Location of places mentioned in this book.
Numbers in brackets refer to page numbers.
Orkney Islands
Kirkwall(32)
Shetland Islands
John O'Groats
Thurso
Wick
Kinloch Bervie
Lewis
The Minch
Dornoch(32)
Ullapool
Moray Firth
Fortrose(32)
Elgin(31)
Fraserburgh
Beauly(31)
Peterhead
Inverness
Outer Hebrides
Inner Hebrides
Skye
Strome Ferry
Loch Ness
Aberdeen(29-30)
Fort Augustus
Balmoral
Braemar
Sea of the Hebrides
Fort William
Brechin(29)
Coll
Dunkeld(38)
Arbroath(29)
Tiree
Dundee(28)
Iona(33)
Mull
Leuchars(25)
Oban
Perth(27)
Dunblane(37)
St Andrews (26)
Dunfermline(24)
Haddington(7)
Stirling(36)
Inchcolm(24)
Whitekirk(7)
Culross(17)
Glasgow(34)
Dalmeny(15)
Kirkliston(16)
Edinburgh(7-13)
Roslin(14)
Pencaitland(6)
Paisley(34)
South Queensferry(16)
Torphicen(17)
Kilwinning(39)
Crichton(14)
Berwick-on-Tweed
Kilmarnock
Kelso(3)
Islay
Ayr
Melrose(5)
Crosraguel(39)
Dumfries
N IRELAND
ENGLAND
Glenluce(39)
Dundrennan Abbey(40)
Whithorn(40)

Morville, Constable of Scotland who received a charter from David I. The canons who came from Alnwick belonged to the Premonstratensian order and were known as White Friars because they wore white habits. The domestic buildings attached to the Abbey were extensive, and following the Reformation had been used as a dwelling house thus being spared the destruction meted out to Roman Catholic establishments at that time. Like the other Border Abbeys the church suffered in the recurring raids.

Excavations carried out by the Ministry of Works in whose care the Abbey is now preserved, revealed that the church consisted of a nave of six bays with vaulted aisles, transepts with chapels, a choir of five bays and a fine central tower. The best preserved parts are the chapels on the north transept, the gable of the south transept and the Norman arched west doorway. The scanty remains of the nave appear to be of a later date - perhaps a 15th. century construction and the cloisters belong to the same period. The soft pink stone with which the Abbey is built makes it specially attractive.

Melrose

Upstream a few miles on a bend of the Tweed with the Eildon Hills in the background, near the site of the Roman fort of Trimontuim stands Melrose Abbey. The Abbey is the successor of a religious house founded by St. Aidan, where St. Cuthbert spent some years as a young man and where his body rested on its way from Lindisfarne when the Danes threatened invasion of the east coast of Northumbria. Monks of the Cistercian Order from Rievault were granted lands from David I for the establishment of a monastery in 1136. Ten years later when only the oratory and living quarters had been built, the Abbey was consecrated and dedicated to the Virgin Mary. As the first Cistercian Abbey in Scotland it received lavish grants from successive kings and nobles throughout its long history. Like the other Border Abbeys it lay in the path of the invader, destroyed in 1322 by Edward II the Abbot and monks were all slain. In 1326 Robert the Bruce granted £2,000 towards its restoration and shortly before his death requested in a letter to his son that his heart be buried in the Abbey. A lifelong desire of the King had been to make a pilgrimage to Jerusalem with the Crusaders. Following his death Lord James Douglas a faithful knight set off on the journey bearing the King's heart in a casket, but he got no further than Spain. Forced to return to Scotland bearing the precious casket, he laid it to rest in Melrose Abbey in fulfilment of the King's request.

The abbey was burned again by Richard II in 1385, and restoration carried out, but the wars of the 16th century caused further destruction to the fabric, and finally the treatment received at the time of the Reformation left the Abbey in ruins. When the abbey was rebuilt in the 15th century it was intended to create it on a larger scale, with additional chapels and finely sculptured decoration.

Yester

From Melrose the traveller can go by way of Lauder and through the Lammermuir Hills to reach East Lothian where there are several interesting churches. The parish churches in the villages are very different from the Border Abbeys. Some are cruciform and others on a T plan. One of the latter type is to be seen at Gifford.

Built in 1710, Yester church dominates this lovely village - the long side of the church facing down the High Street and the shorter sides stretched towards the roads to Haddington and Duns. This simple, whitewashed church is one of the most attractive of this period when far-seeing lairds began to seek suitable sites for new communities at some distance from their mansions. These villages were well planned and usually the church was the focal point as it is at Gifford. Inside the church the laird's loft forms a gallery looking down on the pulpit which stands at the T junction, as if it were indicating the one time influence of the Marquis of Tweeddale over the life of the village.

Pencaitland

Not many miles from Gifford is the village of Pencaitland. The church here is very old, originally dating back to the 13th century. Now greatly altered and added to at various times it still retains some of its early features. It has a 17th century west tower with a fine spire. The least damaged part of the church is the north chapel. The walls of the nave have been rebuilt. There are three sundials in the church, one at the top of the end gable; another on the buttress on the south west and the third is a flat dial on the tower.

Whitekirk

A few miles from Haddington is the 15th century church at Whitekirk once famous for its holy well which made it a place of pilgrimage. It was visited in the 15th century by the priest later to become Pope Pious II. The church is cruciform and has a central tower, with a spire-like roof, built of red free stone and looks very attractive. The church was destroyed in 1914 but later repaired, and is worth a visit.

Haddington

Haddington, the country town of East Lothian is a fascinating place, where there are still old pantiled roofed houses, and dignified with elegant examples of the work of such eminent Scottish architects of the past as William Burn and William Adam. John Knox the great Scots reformer is believed to have been born here, but Gifford makes a similar claim.

The most interesting building in the town is the church of St. Mary which dates back to the 15th century. Known as the Lamp of Lothian on account of its magnificence and eminence in these early days, it still deserves that title today. Between the 15th century and the present day the church has had many ups and downs. During the seige of Haddington the church suffered great destruction, also neglect and decay caused further destruction. Even so the nave continued to be used as a parish church. Cruciform in structure, with a fine square tower, the nave had five bays, the choir with four, both with aisles and a transept without aisles. The central tower with large windows on each face, each with three lights is one of the finest central towers in Scotland. There are also fine carved mouldings and some fascinating gargoyles. A sacristy opening to the north from the choir, is the burial vault of the Earls of Lauderdale. On the way from Haddington to Edinburgh is the tiny, seldom used Seton Church in the grounds of Seton House and only about a mile from the site of the Battle of Prestonpans.

Edinburgh

Edinburgh is a city of churches as though it were a place of pilgrimage' wrote R. L. Stevenson. The capital certainly attracts tourists who admire the unique position of the Castle, explore the famous Royal Mile leading to Holyrood Palace but not all the visitors discover the many interesting churches within its boundaries. It is only possible in this brief study to look at a few of them.

Within the Castle and at the highest point on the rock itself stands the oldest place of worship in Scotland - St. Margaret's Chapel, named after its famous saintly Queen of Malcolm Canmore. Built in 1090 and used by Margaret for her devotions during her residence in the castle shortly before her death in 1093. The Chapel is very small, less than 32 feet by 16 feet, and of a simple rectangular appearance outside but the interior is more ornamental. It has a nave and chancel with a rounded apse within the square east end - the chancel archway is decorated with chevron carving. There are three windows on the south wall one of them in the chancel, a window in each of the end walls. Stained glass of a much later date has been inserted in the windows. The only original stonework lies below the level of the side windows. The arched roof of the nave, built of finely dressed stone is of a much later date. This tiny chapel is still used for special services such as Christenings and the flowers which add to its attractiveness are provided by the Margarets of Scotland.

Greyfriars

On the way down from the Castle looking to the right it is possible to see surrounded by its ancient and celebrated burial ground, Greyfriars, one of the first and largest churches to be built in Edinburgh after the Reformation. In 1561 the city acquired the land for a new graveyard and in 1612 the first church of Greyfriars was built on the site. Its rectangular east-west plan was like that of the nave of a large medieval church, with aisles divided from the main area by arcades making six bays. For the brief period that episcopacy was imposed on Scotland it was raised to a bishopric but reverted to being a parish church after the signing of the National Covenant in the churchyard in 1638.

Cromwell turned the church into a barracks and the damage to the property was extensive, and in 1711 gunpowder stored in the tower caused an explosion which completely destroyed it. The west gable had to be rebuilt, and in 1722 a second place of worship was added to the east-ward and called New Greyfriars. In 1845 Old Greyfriars was so badly burned that only the walls were left. An extensive restoration scheme was carried out in the 1930's, the old and the new churches were made into one again by the removal of the dividing wall. Arcades and aisles were restored giving an unbroken series of arches throughout the entire length of the present Greyfriars Church. Sir Walter Scott attended the church as a boy. When Wesley visited Edinburgh in 1765 he was given a great welcome by the minister of Greyfriars.

St. Giles Cathedral

Only a short distance down the Royal Mile from the castle stands St. Giles Cathedral, whose crown dominates the city sky-line. When Lothian was part of Northumbria, 9th century documents mention the church in Edinburgh as belonging to the diocese of Lindisfarne. Fragments of a later church built by Alexander I around 1120, existed until late in the 18th century. In the ever recurring wars with England, Edinburgh was frequently raided and the church damaged, and in 1385 it was so severely burned that full scale restoration was begun in 1387. When completed the church consisted of a choir of four bays with side aisles, a nave of five bays also having side aisles, a central crossing, north and south transepts and five new chapels added south of the nave. Later on a two bayed chapel known as the Albany Aisle was built on the north-west corner of the nave.

In 1952 this ancient chapel was dedicated as a memorial to members of the congregation of St. Giles who had died in the two world wars and war memorial plaques from other parts of the church were placed within the Albany Aisle, where a lamp of Remembrance burns continuously. During the 15th century wealthy merchants in the city provided funds to extend the church, the centre aisle was heightened, the vaulting renewed, the transepts were lengthened and a bay was added to the choir. The north column of this new bay is called the Kings' pillar for its capital is decorated with four shields - those of James II and his consort Mary of Guelders, James III and the Fleur-de-Lys of France, Scotland's staunch ally at this period. About the middle of the 15th century when a relic of St. Giles - an arm bone - was received from Bruges by Sir William Preston, a private chapel of three bays bearing his name, was added south of the choir aisle. During the upheaval at the Reformation the relic was lost but this magnificent shrine with its fine vaulting and heraldic decoration still stands. In the south-east corner of the Preston Aisle is the Chepman Aisle named after the man who introduced printing into Scotland and who was buried in the chapel in 1532. St. Giles suffered greatly at the time of the Reformation and after the disturbances were over the church was thought too large. It was divided up into several places of worship and for a brief spell became an Episcopal church. Luckenbooths clustered against the walls, the General Assembly met in the Preston Aisle, and the town clerk had offices within the church. When in 1829 alterations and reconstruction took place the building contained three churches, but between 1872-83 the interior was finally restored to become one church - the High Kirk of Edinburgh. The ancient and historic chapels combine happily with more recent features like the beautiful stained glass windows and the magnificent Chapel of the Knights of the Thistle built as recently as 1909-1911 at the south-east corner of the Cathedral.

Canongate

Further down the Royal Mile is the Canongate Church, the building of which came about in a strange way. The inhabitants of the Canongate district, who worshipped in Holyrood Abbey were deprived of this privelege, when James II and VII decreed that the Abbey was to become the chapel of the Order of the Thistle. A new church had to be built and Thomas Moodie of Saughtonhall, a rich merchant, left the money for this purpose. The site chosen was in the middle of the Canongate on the north side.

Building began in 1688, the year of James' death and the style of the church is extremely simple the street front gable Dutch curvilinear with round headed windows. In the apse is a Gothic window and the well proportioned arcading between the nave and the aisles is supported by Tuscan columns, while the transepts are spanned by semicircular arches. The Royal Arms appear on the front gable and on the topmost point the carved head of a deer with a cross between its antlers symbolising the legend of of the Holyrood.

During restoration in 1950 a tiny semi-circular apse discovered behind where the organ stood was incorporated within the church. The close association with royalty has been maintained since its foundation at the command of James II and when George IV came to Edinburgh in 1822 the commissioners of the General Assembly met in the Canongate Church before going to Holyrood to be presented to the King. A few years ago Her Majesty the Queen as a parishoner and seat holder exercised her right of worshipping there during a state visit to Scotland.

Holyrood Abbey

Beside the Palace of Holyrood House, where the Queen stays during state visits to Scotland, stand the ruins of Holyrood Abbey founded by King David in 1128, as an Augustinian house for canons from St. Andrews. The Palace was not built until 1498 but James I used the Abbey as a royal residence in 1425. Both Palace and Abbey were damaged by fire in 1544 and 1547, and again accidentally by Cromwell in 1650.

The earliest church on the site was a small cruciform building, some of which still forms part of the nave, but most of the remainder dates from the 13th century. Originally the church had a choir of six bays and a nave with eight, both with aisles. There was a central tower, north transept with eastern chapels and two western towers. The cloister was on the south side of the nave, with an octagonal chapter-house on its east side. The present palace stands on the site of the monastic buildings.

The choir in a ruinous state was demolished in 1569 and the stones were used to turn the nave into the parish church of the Canongate. Further decay and destruction followed but of what remains the details on the west front are the most interesting with fine arcading. On the north side of the nave the flying buttresses added in the 15th century are most impressive. The oldest surviving part is the 12th century south wall, with a fine Romanesque doorway at the east end and original arcading along the wall. The flying buttresses here are carried right to the ground being carried over the cloister roof on arches, with a further tier connecting them with the clerestory. This structure was so effective that it withstood the collapse of the roof.

Although little remains of the magnificence of this great Abbey, the Royal Vault at the south-east corner of the nave contains the remains of many Scottish Kings, David II, James II and his Queen, James V and Darnley, husband of Mary Queen of Scots. What may seem a rather neglected ruin has a glory all its own which impresses the visitor.

Duddingston

Although within the city Duddingston Kirk occupies an almost pastoral setting overlooking a loch at the foot of Arthurs Seat. The church dates back to Norman times and for almost four hundred years was associated with the Abbey of Kelso, later it came under the diocese of St. Andrews but following the Reformation it was placed under the care of the minister of Holyrood. Throughout the centuries the church has changed but the Romanesque south doorway and chancel arch remain, the two scenes of the Passion carved on the shaft of the doorway are much weathered but the chevron decoration of the chancel is still clearly visible.

The original church consisted of a nave and chancel, a north transept erected in 1631 to allow seating for the family and tenants of Sir James Hamilton of Priestfield, was thought to have spoiled the simplicity of the early church. Perhaps the best known of the ministers of Duddingston Church was John Thomson also an artist of considerable merit who entertained at the manse the more distinguished painters Sir David Wilkie and Turner. Among the Elders in his congregation was Sir Walter Scott who is said to have written part of the Heart of Midlothian in the manse garden.

At the entrance gate to the church can be seen fixed to the wall - 'jougs', an iron collar in two halves fastened by a clasp. The jougs were placed round the necks of offenders in punishment for petty crimes. Also outside the Kirk is a 'loupin stane' a stone platform with a few steps leading up to it, from which church attenders could mount the horses on which they had ridden to the service.

Restalrig

Not very far from the Meadowbank Sports Stadium is the interesting old parish church of Restalrig. Legend has it that St. Triduan died at Restalrig in 510 and that the well has healing properties. It became a place of pilgrimage and a church existed there from the 12th century and in 1296 the 'Pastor of Restalric' swore allegiance to Edward I. In 1487, Pope Innocent raised Restalrig to a collegiate foundation, one of four such churches in Edinburgh. James III died before carrying out his intention of making Restalrig a Chapel Royal but James IV made provision for a dean and canon with eight prebendaries. He also arranged for the upkeep of a chaplain, but the Battle of Flodden robbed the parish of its royal benefactor and the landowner of Restalrig, Sir John Logan. In 1515 James V endowed the church with lands and until the Reformation it flourished greatly. Then the holy well was filled up and all except the chancel of the church was destroyed. In 1836 restoration was carried out and it is now the parish church of the area. In the church-yard still stands a small hexagonal building which may have been the chapel house of the old church or chapel of St. Triduan. It has a fine vaulted roof with some splendid carved bosses.

Corstorphine

In the western suburb of Corstorphine stands a fine 15th century church built on the site of a chapel founded by David I. At the end of the 14th century Sir Adam Forrester one time Provost of Edinburgh, Chamberlain to Queen Annabella and Keeper of the Great Seal acquired lands in Corstorphine and built a chapel which was dedicated in 1404 to St. John the Baptist. This chapel is the chancel of the present building.

Sir Adam's son John became Lord High Chancellor of Scotland and for services rendered to his sovereign was granted a charter by James I 'for the maintenance of three chaplains for divine service in the chapel of St. John of Corstorphine'. Sir John Forrester added the low tower with octagonal spire, one of the most striking feature of the church as it is today. With the passage of time additions and reconstructions have taken place, making it look like a group of small buildings, with flag stone roofs and gables.

However when in 1905 a genuine restoration was undertaken original doorways were replaced and an arcade of three arches was built separating the nave and aisle. In the church are the three generations of Forrester tombs, two in arched recesses are of recumbent life-size figures clad in mail, and the third is in the South transept. Other interesting features are the alter built in below the east window, the piscinas in the chancel and the North Sacristy, a fine sedilia and a number of coats of arms carved on the outside. It is a sturdy and dignified building retaining the peaceful atmosphere of a village church in the midst of the bustle of the city.

Crichton

Within easy reach of Edinburgh, there are a few churches worthy of a visit and the first of these stands on the slopes of the Moorfoot Hills. Crichton Church, built of pink sandstone, is a neat compact building with large windows in three gables giving it plenty of light inside. It is a 15th century cruciform church with barrel-vaulting and a low central tower, having a saddled backed roof within a corbelled parapet, and at the top of the east gable is a tiny bell-cot.

The nave was never completed but the north wall extends westwards beyond the tower and contains a spiral stair. The transepts differ in size. The T shape of the church made it very suitable for the Reformed style of worship for the pulpit was placed against the west end with the seating arranged to face towards it. Among the original features inside the church are the sedilia on the south side of the chancel, a much restored aumbry, and the fine flower carvings on the capitals of the piers of the crossing are almost the only decoration on this very plain interior.

Crichton Church was closely associated with the Crichton family, the ruins of whose castle stands a short distance from the church. Its founder Sir William Crichton, chancellor to James II was partly responsible for the Black Dinner at which members of the Douglas family were murdered in the presence of the young king in Edinburgh Castle.

Roslin

Roslin Chapel has been described as 'the most remarkable and ornate flamboyant Gothic building in Britain'. It is certainly a unique and most attractive church - intended to be on the grand scale but only the choir with aisles and a sunk eastern sacristy were completed. It was founded in 1446 by Sir William St. Clair, Earl of Orkney as a collegiate establishment of a provost, six prebendaries and two singing bays are dedicated to St. Matthew.

Like Crichton, Roslin Chapel occupies an attractive site. It overlooks the River North Esk and is within easy reach of Roslin Castle, the one time seat of the St. Clairs, very wealthy landowners with property in Orkney, Fife and Midlothian.

The chapel consists of a choir with north and south

aisles connected by an aisle running across the east end and leads to four chapels beyond it to the east. The design is fairly symmetrical, the bays all of the same dimensions, but varying in the design of the carvings. All the buttresses rise in unbroken lines to the wall heads of the aisles where a cornice continues round them. Two rows of square and oblong pinnacles decorated with carved rosettes and crockets add to the attractive appearance of the outside. The north and south doorways are recessed in mock porches made by round arches thrown between the buttresses. The windows of the aisles are all of two lights and of those in the eastern chapels four have the engrailed cross of the St. Clairs wrought into the tracery.

But, it is the inside which is so unusual. The arches and capitals of all the pillars are richly carved. The sculpture which adorns the chapel mainly depicts scripture scenes. Symbols of the seven deadly sins and the seven virtues appear on bands on the lintels. Groups of figures from the Passion are carved on the north and south doorways and a row of apostles can be seen on an arch in the south aisle and on the outside of a north window. Although most of the carving is Scottish, the apostles suggest French inspiration. The most famous of all the carvings in the chapel is on the south pillar on the east aisle, known as the Prentice Pillar and legend has it, the work of an apprentice whose jealous master slew him when he saw the beauty of the work carried out while he was absent, (searching for ideas worthy of the beautiful chapel). The decoration consists of a series of carved wreaths curving from base to capital round on quarter of the pillar; a real masterpiece in this exceedingly attractive chapel.

Dalmeny

Perhaps the finest example of Romanesque church architecture in Scotland can be seen at Dalmeny, on Lord Rosebery's estate. Standing on the village green this lovely little parish church has been in continuous use since the 12th century. The plan is simple, consisting of a semi-circular apse, tiny chancel, and a rather dark nave, vaulted at the east end. The few windows are very narrow but have fine chevron decoration round the openings and a splendid Norman arch divides the sanctuary from the 'body of the Kirk'. The south doorway, is particularly worth seeing for the grotesque carved decoration is masterly, having over it a panel of interlacing arches forming blank arcading. The rather squat tower, although added during recent restorations, is quite in keeping with the plain plan of this charming place of worship.

Kirkliston

A few miles from Dalmeny is another old church which although much altered and modernised, has a fine 12th. century west tower, one of the few in Scotland of the period with buttresses. Two fine doorways also survive from these early times. The 17th century bell-cot on the eastern gable is most attractive. In the church can be seen the memorial to Scott's 'Bride of Lammermuir'.

Carmelite Friars Church

Almost at the waters edge in the little town of South Queensferry named after the saintly Queen Margaret of Scotland, stands the Friary Church of St. Mary of Mount Carmel. It was at this point that the body of Queen Margaret was shipped across for her burial at Dunfermline Abbey after she had died at Edinburgh Castle in 1093. This little church is the only medieval Carmelite church still in use as a place of worship in Britain. The Carmelites came to Scotland in 1260 but the house of the order at Queensferry was not founded until 1330 by the Laird of Dundas, but the earliest charter granting lands is dated 1475, after which the church was built.

The monks were dispersed at the time of the Reformation but by 1584 a Royal Charter returned the lands to the Dundas family. In 1635 the Episcopalians built the present church but as time went by the buildings deteriorated. As the church stands today the choir remains with a low tower to the west. Southwards from the tower is a transept and westward is an arch which led to the nave, demolished about seventy years ago.

Linlithgow

In few places can buildings of church and state be seen together in such a fine setting as the ancient Palace of Linlithgow and the parish church of St. Michael. Situated beside the loch the massive ruins of the famous palace in no way lessen the impressive dignity of the church. One of the largest of the ancient Scottish churches, it is less altered than most, and even when part of it was partitioned off for use, the unused area was maintained by a wise town council. Happily the dividing wall has been removed and the church restored in a most satisfactory way.

The outside of the church is very attractive, with niches on the buttresses, large windows with well designed tracery, the gable of the apse finished with crow steps, and the parapet of the south aisle of the choir has plain gargoyles designed to throw the water off the windows. The square tower is finished with battlements and corner turrets, and in recent years a gilded spiky crown has been added which seems rather incongruous.

The plan of the church is made up of a choir of three bays with aisles, a three sided apse to the east, a nave of five bays and aisles, with access from a south porch doorway, two chapels, in place of transepts, containing upper floor rooms, and a west tower. The aisles, transept chapels and the porch are vaulted. There are small triforium openings in the nave and a stone bench runs along the walls of the nave aisles and extend into the transept chapels. Legend has it that it was in the south chapel, which is dedicated to St. Michael, that an apparition appeared to James IV warning him to the fatal campaign of Flodden.

Torphicen

Four miles south of Linlithgow stands the ruins of the church of the Preceptory of the Knights of St. John. The upper stories of the tower and transepts have rooms with fireplaces no doubt used as part of the 'hospital' associated with the Order. More like a castle than a church it consisted of a long narrow choir and nave, with transepts and a high central tower. On the original nave now stands the parish church of Torphicen, and uninteresting 18th century building which seems to endow the stark simplicity of the earlier with a peculiar dignity.

Culross Abbey

On the north side of the Forth, high above the charming old town of Culross, stands the site of a 12th century Cistercian Abbey. Only one wall of the early church still remains but of the restoration carried out in the reign of James IV the choir and tower can still be seen. On the tower are the arms of Abbot Masoun who flourished between 1498-1513. The choir is the parish church of the town and in the north transept is the elaborate alabaster tomb of Sir George Bruce of Carnock, 'a worthy burgher' whose invention of machinery to drain the coal workings under the Forth earned him the Knighthood conferred on

Melrose Abbey, see page 5

St. Margaret's Chapel, Edinburgh Castle See page 8

Dornock Cathedral, See page 32

St. Andrews Cathedral at St. Andrews, see page 26

Kelso Abbey See page 3

Entrance to Kelso Abbey, see page 3

Canongate Church, Edinburgh See page 10

him by James I and VI while on a visit to Culross.

The manse occupies the site of some of the monastic buildings on the west side of the cloister. To the south of the house are remains of the rooms occupied by lay brethern. The doorway of the chapter house still stands and excavations carried out by the office of works have unearthed much of the foundations of the old Abbey. Also in the same area is an old parish church with some interesting tombstones and to the east of the town foundations of a church to St. Mungo dating from the 15th century, cruciform in style with an eastern apse.

Dunfermline

At the time of the Norman Conquest, Dunfermline was the capital of the Pictish kingdom of Scotland and it was there that Malcolm Canmore married the refugee Princess Margaret of England. The new Queen was deeply religious and her biographer Turgot tells that soon after the wedding she founded a church 'in that place where the nuptials were celebrated'. The foundations of this church, dedicated to the Holy Trinity in 1074, were uncovered during excavations in 1917. The original burial place of Queen Margaret was revealed at the east end of the nave. The Abbey church was built by David I and dedicated in 1150, and the Queen's remains were reinterred there by her son. It was a large and magnificent church of which only the nave has survived in anything like its original state, alongside the foundations of the monastic buildings which were connected to the ancient royal palace, by a vaulted gatehouse. King Charles I was born in the palace and Charles II visited it.

Inchcolm Abbey

On the tiny island of Inchcolm off shore from Aberdour in the Firth of Forth stands the most complete monastic remains in Scotland. From early Christian times it was greatly favoured as a burial place and Shakespeare refers to this in Macbeth when he writes of the defeat of Sweno:
'Nor would be deign him burial of his men;
Till he disbursed, at Saint Colm's inch,
Ten thousand dollars to our general use.'

The foundation of the Abbey is a romantic story. Alexander I driven ashore in a fierce storm on the island sought refuge in the cave of a hermit who shared his scanty fare with the king and his men. As a thank offering for the

saving of his life Alexander founded and endowed the Abbey
in 1123, as an Augustinian house. Although on an island
the Abbey suffered severe damage from attacks by the
English Fleet in the Wars of Independence. The church
buildings fell into decay but the monk's quarters were
taken over at the Reformation by the Morays of Aberdour
and turned into a private residence. Still in a fine state of
preservation it is now under the care of the Department of
the Environment. The first church was Romanesque but
later was replaced by a large Gothic cruciform building.
The 13th century chapter house octagonal in form, and
stone-roofed, has a stone bench running all along the walls
where the monks sat.

Leuchars

The exceedingly fine Norman church at Dalmeny has
already been described, the old part of the parish church
of Leuchars is equally worthy of note. H.V. Morton
likened it 'to a Norman Knight on horseback' and a distinguished architect considered the chancel and apse one of
the finest fragments of the Romanesque style to be found
in Britain. At least a chapel existed which was handed
over to St. Andrews in 1187. The de Quincys, local landowners and doughty Crusaders were responsible for the
completion of the church, symbolic crosses decorating
the sanctuary arch commemorate the crusades. Only the
chancel and apse remain but in an exceptionally fine state
of preservation.

On the outside is richly decorated arcading with chevron
pattern. Carved corbels run along below the roof and
above the apse is a curious 17th century bell-turret which
somehow does not spoil the perfection of the Romanesque
features.

The interior also has rich chevron carving the chancel
arch is particularly fine and has vaulting with heavy moulded groins and simple cushion caps of short single shafts
resting on grotesque heads. The lower part of the apse is
plain, a string course with faceted decoration separating
it from the moulded window arches above. The later
additions to the church in no way detract from the perfection of the Romanesque portion, for both parts blend harm-
oniously together. Leuchars was favoured with a visit
from the great Dr. Johnson in 1763.

St. Andrews-St. Leonards

The peaceful old town of St. Andrews has a long history, both academic and ecclesiastical. It has the oldest University in Scotland and before the Reformation was the ecclesiastical equivalent of Canterbury. Although the university does not come into this study the old churches are bound up with its history. In 1144 a hospital once administered by the Culdees was put in care of the Augustinian canons attached to the Cathedral priory by the Bishop of St. Andrews. The hospital of St. Leonard sheltered pilgrims to the shrine of St. Andrew and would have had a chapel attached to it. By 1413 it had become a parish church and was also used as a meeting place by the new first university, and in 1544 the College of St. Leonard became the Arts and Theology faculty.

Difficult times in the 18th century led to the union of St. Leonard's College with St. Salvators in 1747 as twin arts colleges. The following year St. Leonards College residential buildings passed into private hands but the church, although in a poor state, was not included in the sale 'in case it shall ever be repaired and again used as a church'. Its derelict state was caustically commented upon by Dr. Johnson but since then the university authorities have replaced the roof and put in windows. It stands within the area of one of the most famous girls schools in Scotland.

St. Salvators

St. Salvators College was founded in 1456 by Bishop Kennedy and the church was the college chapel. The plan was rectangular with a three sided apse at the east end with windows in each side, the centre one larger than the others. There were no windows in the north and west walls but the south divided by buttresses with seven bays had a large pointed window in each bay. The gabled pinnacles on the buttresses are a modern replacement of a more stunted design. A porch is formed by two buttresses with stone benches running along the sides. The tower is characteristically Scottish in form and at the foot a gateway with the arms of Bishop Kennedy above it leads to the grounds of the College. Inside the church is the memorial erected by the Bishop. To the right of the memorial is a sacristy with the Royal Arms and those of Bishop Kennedy.

St. Andrews Cathedral

Legend surrounds the choice of St. Andrew as patron saint of Scotland but it is said that relics of St. Andrew were brought from the church bearing his name in Hexham. The bishopric dates from the 10th century and a priory of Augustinian canons was founded in 1120. Nothing is left of the conventual buildings erected at that time but what remains of the church of St. Regulus occupies the site of the old priory.

The building of the cathedral - the largest church of its time in Scotland - was begun in 1160. The extensive lands of the university were enclosed by a wall with 'Pends' - a large gatehouse opening into the priory grounds from the medieval town. Little is now left of the great 'metropolitan cathedral of all Scotland'. The foundations of the church and convent have been excavated and the whole area which is beautifully kept provides a restful retreat from the busy town surrounding it. Still standing are the east gable, part of the west one, parts of the walls of the south aisle of the nave and the west wall of the south transept. Throughout its history the cathedral was altered and restored but finally fell into ruin. What remains of the monastic buildings is very fine especially the chapterhouse and refectory. There is a museum of sculptured stones and memorial slabs found during the excavations. The whole setting is so fine that a visit to the cathedral remains is well worth while.

St. John the Baptist

In the county town of Perth, early residence of the Scottish Kings, it is disappointing to find that little remains of the many monastic buildings that once existed. The only one to be seen now is the church of St. John the Baptist, and it has been altered and restored so often that little of the early structure remains. First mention of a church on the site appears in a Charter dated between 1124-1127, granted by David I and associated with the Abbey of Dunfermline. The church dedicated to St. John the Baptist was consecrated in 1242 by the Bishop of St. Andrews. In time the building deteriorated and repairs were carried out under orders from Robert the Bruce in 1328. At the time of the Reformation it was stripped of all adornment and divided by sturdy walls into three separate places or worship. The walls have been removed and the building restored to become the Perthshire War Memorial.

The church consists of nave and choir each of five bays with aisles, a north porch, central tower and spire. The spire is old and the tower parapet is battlemented. One most interesting part is the north porch known as Halkerston's Tower, so called after John Halkerston who was master of works to Queen Mary of Guelders. He may well have been responsible for the vaulting of the nave of the church between 1461-69. Standing as it does in the centre of the town it is not seen to advantage.

Dundee

Dundee has the unique distinction of having the largest and finest church tower in Scotland, now all that remains of the ancient parish church, which dated back to the 15th century. The tower is at the west of the original church on the site of which now exists three separate congregation under one roof. St. Mary's occupies the former choir area, old St. Pauls the transept and St. Clements the nave. The lower part of the tower contains the west doorway of St. Clements and consists of two rounded arches within an eliptical arch. The arch mouldings are decorated with carved foliage, the jambs and central pillar moulded with alternate rounds and hollows. In the spandrel over the central pillar is a circular panel enclosing a carving of the Virgin and Child and below on a shield the arms of the Diocese of Brechin.

Arbroath Abbey

On an exposed part of the coast, some miles north east of Dundee, stands Arbroath now a popular holiday resort, and an important fishing port which is dominated by the massive ruins of its ancient abbey. Like Kelso it was a Feronesian house of the Benedictine order, founded by William the Lion on his return from captivity in 1176 and dedicated to St. Mary and Thomas a Becket - murdered in Canterbury only four years earlier. The building was sufficiently well advanced to allow the King to be buried in the presbytery in 1214 and the completed abbey was dedicated in 1233.

The church consisted of a choir of three bays, a presbytery, a nave of nine bays, north and south transepts, all with aisles. There was a central and two western towers. There were also extensive monastic buildings attached to the church. Only fragments of this large and important ecclesiastical settlement remain but these are most impressive, particularly the large deeply recessed doorway set in a round arch on the west front. The south wall of the transept has elaborate three tier arcading, topped by tall pointed arched windows, but it is the circular windows in the gable above these which is the dominating feature of the old Abbey.

Brechin Cathedral

Like so many Scottish ecclesiastical buildings Brechin Cathedral has suffered greatly at the hands of the restorers, and little of the original church is to be seen. Fortunately the most interesting feature still stands at the south-west corner of the cathedral. This is an 11th century round tower, one of three in Scotland belonging to the Celtic church period. The conical roof is a later addition. The carving round the doorway, which is well above ground level, resembles similar structures in Ireland. The bishopric of Brechin was founded by David I but nothing remains of the church built in his time. The 15th century west tower has been incorporated in the 19th century restoration, and the western parts of the choir, the arcade and clerestory, fine examples of 13th century work, can still be seen.

St. Machars Cathedral

In old Aberdeen are two specially interesting churches, St. Machars' Cathedral and Kings College Chapel, the cathedral 12th century and the chapel 16th. Like so many famous churches, the first Christian settlement on the site was by the Celtic disciples of St. Columba, and it was Machar who came to Aberdeen about 580. The traditional story of its beginning is depicted in six scenes in a stained glass window erected as a memorial to John Crombie, killed in 1917 and carried out by Douglas Strachan. A Norman church stood on the site when in 1136 David I raised it to a bishopric and in 1357 work was started on what was to be a great cathedral. Of this ambitious plan only two sandstone pillars at the east end remain. Bishop Henry de Lichton 1423-40 completed the western towers and laid the foundations for the nave and the great central tower - which was not completed until 1512 and collapsed in a storm in 1688 as the result of some of the buttresses being removed to erect barracks during the Cromwellian period. No attempt has been made since to rebuild it.

The choir was also built in the early part of the 16th century but was destroyed in 1560 and all evidence of its existence has now been removed.

The west front, all except the spires on the twin towers, built of warm pink tinted granite seems to lessen the severity of the design. The window above the west door has seven long round headed lights with stained glass dating from 1867, and depicting Christ and his disciples, with small insets showing how they met their deaths. The south door now the main entrance to the church has a porch with stone seats along the sides where it is said beggars sat soliciting alms. The nave consisting of eight bays and aisles has a flat ceiling of oak, put in at the expense of Bishop Dunbar in 1520. The work of James Winter it is decorated with heraldic shields bearing the arms of James V and the Scottish nobles of his time, archbishops and bishops, Pope Leo X and reigning Kings of Europe - a fine memorial to both carver and Bishop.

Kings College Chapel

The west end of Kings College Chapel with its attractive tower faces the main street of old Aberdeen and occupies the north west corner of the university quadrangle. The inscription over the west doorway states that the chapel was founded in 1500 by King James IV. The plan is rectangular with a three sided apse at the east end, the tower is in line with the west end but projects from the south wall. It is divided into six bays with projecting buttresses having large windows with mullions and tracery in each bay on the north side except one which contains a doorway. The windows round the apse are also large, so too is the one over the west doorway which has four lights, with mullions and loop tracery enclosed by a round arch. Most of the windows have the pointed arch of the period. Four buttresses similar to those on the chapel, support the corners of the tower which is capped by a crown lantern, not the original one, but a very attractive replacement giving the building a distinctive air. In contrast to St. Machars, Kings College Chapel is built of sandstone. Like the cathedral it has some fine woodwork the finest being the rood screen.

Pluscardine Priory

The story of Pluscardine is unusual and interesting for it flourishes again today after many changes of fortune.

Orginally, a Benedictine community, founded by Alexander II in 1230 and later in 1453-4 united with the priory of Urquhart when both had too few monks to maintain a separate establishment.

After the Reformation the monastery was deserted but early in this century two Carthusian monks came from France with a view to acquiring the premises. The prohibitive cost of reinstating the monastic buildings deterred them.

In 1920 Lord Calum Crichton-Stuart offered the Priory to the Benedictines of Caldey Island in South Wales but they were unable to accept then - or at a later date when the offer was renewed. In 1948 Lord Calum appealed to Prinknash Abbey for a group of monks to renew the abbey and they accepted and sent six monks to occupy the remains of the ancient priory. Through dedicated faith and much hard work a wonderful restoration has taken place and Pluscardine Priory is once again a Benedictine community.

Elgin Cathedral

The Cathedral church of the Holy Trinity in Elgin, much of it late 13th century, is an outstanding example of Gothic architecture in Scotland, and compares very favourably with its European contemporaries. It was one of the most perfect cathedrals, having a large nave with double aisles, an extended choir and presbytery, north and south transepts, a lady chapel and an octagonal chapter house, standing apart from the main part of the church. Although in ruins, enough remains to testify to the splendour so frequently referred to by historians. The west front is most impressive and emphasises French influence with its twin square towers with deep buttresses and rather small windows. One west doorway, one of the finest in Scotland, has nine circular shafts and mouldings, the inner part of the doorway having two smaller arches and tympanum all richly decorated with carvings belongs to a later date than the outer section.

Beauly Priory

The traveller to the far north of Scotland will find few ancient churches to explore but in a few places are the remains of early monastic settlements. At Beauly are the ruins of the Cistercian priory founded by Alexander II in 1230.

The plan of the church is simple, built without aisles,

the nave is long with short transepts also without aisles and the choir is a continuation of the nave. The transept chapels are walled off from the main part of the church and the north chapel is vaulted. In the choir is a double piscina, a feature only found in 13th century churches. The west door is of good design, the round headed doorway with mouldings but no capitals on the shafts. The church is roofless and the remains are in the care of the Department of the Environment.

Fortrose Cathedral

At Fortrose Cathedral, in Ross-shire also looked after by the Department of the Environment only foundations and lower walls and the vaulted south aisle and turret stairway can now be seen. The rib-vaulting of the south aisle, with traverse ridge-ribs at right angles to the walls is typical of the English style of the 14th century and rare in Scotland. Evidence of the fine large windows is still visible, but the tracery has gone and there is an interesting pointed arch doorway.

Dornoch Cathedral

Dornoch Cathedral has been destroyed and rebuilt more than once and is now the parish church of the little town of Dornoch in Sutherlandshire. Little of the early building remains but the church as it stands now is well worth a visit. It has some interesting stained glass windows inserted during recent restoration.

St. Magnus Cathedral, Kirkwall

The magnificent red sandstone cathedral of St. Magnus in Kirkwall has been described as 'the most splendid monument left by the Norse occupation of our northern isles'. When it was founded in 1137 by the crusader Earl Rognvald in memory of the saintly Earl Magnus, the Orkney Islands belonged to Norway and the cathedral came under the diocese of Trondheim. It was not until 1468 that the islands became part of Scotland and the cathedral became subject to the Bishop of St. Andrews.

The earliest part of the cathedral to be erected was the east end and by the middle of the 12th century the choir and transepts had been completed. The choir was lengthened at a later date. The west front with its much weathered, Norman doorway stands facing the main street of the town. Although smaller than most famous cathedrals, it appears very spacious when viewed from the west door. The solid round pillars are surmounted by the semi-circular arches of the arcade. The arches of the triforum are also semi-circular but those of the clerestory are pointed, giving the choir and nave a lofty and dignified appearance. Along the walls of the nave is interlaced arcading resting on pillars in groups of four. Between two of these is a plaque to the memory of those who lost their lives when the Royal Oak sank in Scapa Flow in the 1939-45 war. The east window has four lights with pointed arches over which is a fine circular window with tracery. Within cavities in opposite pillars in the north arcade of the choir are interred relics of the founder St. Rognvald first discovered during restoration in the 18th century. The remains of St. Magnus came to light in 1919 and it is believed that they were hidden in the pillar for safety at the time of the Reformation.

Iona

Of the thirteen cathedrals in Scotland Iona occupies a unique position, both territorially and historically. It was on the island of Iona off the coast of Mull in the west of Scotland that St. Columba landed in 563, when he fled from Ireland. There he founded a monastery which became the largest and most famous of the Celtic churches of the time. Little remains of the monastery but a number of sculptured stones and splendid Celtic crosses have survived, two of these called St. John's cross and St. Martin's cross stand in the grounds of the restored cathedral, a reminder of its long history and importance in Celtic times. Iona has been a place of pilgrimage since the days of St. Columba when it established itself as a centre of learning and missionary enterprise.

The first church may have been a timber construction. However in 1203 the Benedictine Abbey of Iona was founded under diocese of Dunkeld and when transferred to the Bishopric of the Island it became a cathedral. Much of the monastic quarters and the north transept date back to the 13th century but most of what exists today was built in the 16th century. Like so many other fine churches its fabric deteriorated through neglect following the Reformation. Not until 1910 was the restoration on a large scale undertaken. At that time the nave and south choir aisle were rebuilt and the whole church roofed. Since then other areas have been renewed and it is hoped that one day the entire restoration of the monastic settlement will be completed.

The cathedral is a very plain, cruciform in plan having a sturdy low tower with square windows one each side, three of them with fine tracery. The warm pink of the walls is attractive and the large windows of the presbytery and in the gables of the transepts give light to the inside. The capitals of the piers in the south choir aisle and the crossing have very interesting Celtic carvings depicting hunting scenes, flowers and beasts as well as sculptural subjects.

Glasgow Cathedral

For fifteen centuries the site on which St. Mungo's Cathedral in Glasgow stands, has been hallowed ground. St. Ninian is reported to have built a church there in the beginning of the 5th century. St. Mungo who revived religion in the 6th century is said to have founded an apiscopal see, and dedicated the church to the Holy Trinity. It was he who brought Fergus for burial in a spot now covered by the Blacader Aisle in the present church. St. Mungo and St. Columba are believed to have met and exchanged pastoral staffs in the early place of worship. Between this time and the religious revival in the time of the saintly Queen Margaret, little is known of what went on, but her son David restored the See of Glasgow in 1115 and appointed his tutor bishop.

A new church built on the old site was consecrated in 1136 in the presence of King David and his court. This church was destroyed by fire but rebuilt and dedicated in 1197. Only a fragment of this church remains near the south-west entrance to the Lower Church.

The building that exists today was begun by Bishop William de Bondington (1333-58) in whose lifetime the Quire and Lower Church were completed. The nave was not finished until the beginning of the 14th century. Work continued throughout the next two centuries and Archbishop Blacader, 1483-1508, was responsible for the addition of the beautiful aisle which now bears his name, and the impressive Quire screen. The fact that the ground falls away steeply towards the river gave the builders the opportunity of exercising their skill in creating the very fine lower church or crypt with its exceedingly fine vaulting, among the best in Scotland, which contains St. Mungo's shrine.

The cathedral suffered during the unrest of the 16th century and following the Reformation it was, like so many other Scottish churches, stripped of its beautiful furnishings and its altars destroyed. By some good fortune its walls and roof stood and worship continued unbroken for almost seven hundred years. Although the cathedral is now in the care of the Department of the Environment as an ancient monument services of the Church of Scotland are held in the choir area.

Paisley Abbey

Paisley Abbey was founded in 1169 when the High Steward of Scotland invited the Prior of Wenlock Abbey to establish a priory of the Cluniac Order of Benedictines on an island in the Clyde known as Kings Inch. There was already an ancient church dedicated to the Irish 6th century St. Mirenus so that when the priory church was built the original saint was included in the consecration as well as St. Milburga, patron of the monks of Wenlock, St. James patron saint of the Stewarts and the Blessed Virgin. The connection with the Stewart family continued up to the marriage of Walter to Marjory, daughter of Robert the Bruce, and the Stewarts became kings of Scotland. The Stuart kings up to the time of Robert III were buried within the abbey, but all that can be seen today is a recumbent female figure on a tomb believed to be that of Marjory Bruce. In 1245 the priory was raised to abbey status, but like so many Scottish monasteries it suffered waves of destruction during the repeated conflicts with England.

Restorations were carried out time and again but finally the Reformation put an end to the monastic settlement. The oldest part dating from 1499 in St. Mirens Chapel situated at the south end of the south transept. The chapel has two vaults above it, with a chamber between. The frieze of figures in bas-relief on the east wall illustrate the life of St. Miren. Four steps lead up to the sanctuary area of the chapel and therein burns a light, a rare thing in Scottish churches.

The oldest areas of the church are the eastern section of the south aisle and the lower part of the west front containing a fine doorway with side arcading. The upper parts are of a later date consisting of two tall three light windows with a single window above of an even later period. The clerestory and triforum resemble those in the choir at

Glasgow and may have been modelled on them. The triforum has semi-circular arches of the same width as those of the arcade. The clerestory is unusual in that the passage way does not run inside the shafts dividing the bays but passes along the outside of the shafts on a series of corbelled projections. This produces a rather heavy look as seen from the floor of the church.

The Church of Holy Rood, Stirling

The church of the Holy Rood in Stirling is large and impressive standing on the Castle Hill with its apse making a very striking feature at the head of St. Johns Wynd. A strongly French influence is evident throughout the building but mostly noticeable in the lofty chancel and apse. The tower in the centre of the west end is battlemented so also is the parapet of the apse.

The nave is 15th century with cylindrical piers resembling those of the Romanesque period. The choir which is 16th century is very fine and spacious with clustered piers having continuous straight mouldings over the capitals. Both choir and nave have vaulted aisles. Only one of the three original chantry chapels opening from the nave remains on the north side. This small attractive vaulted chapel, named after St. Andrew, has a ribbed and groined vault with coats of arms on the bosses, windows to the north and west and a stone bench on the west side.

Inchmahome Priory

On a small island in the Lake of Menteith stand the ruins of the priory of Inchmahome - whose name means Isle of Rest and it is a truly restful place. In an area where there are very few noteworthy ancient churches, Inchmahome provided much of interest in its history.

The priory was established for the Augustinian order by the 4th Earl of Mentieth in 1238. The church and the monastic buildings were very fine but following the Reformation, the living quarters were demolished and the stones used to build a castle for the Earls on another islet on the lake. Fortunately the 13th century church survived and although roofless is fairly complete, consisting of a choir without aisles, a nave of four bays, a north aisle and a tower of a later period rising from the west bay of the aisle. There was a sacristy on the north of the choir and on the south side a cloister-walk ran along the length of the church. By far the finest feature of the building is the large west door with a deeply moulded arch head and two blind arches on each side. The great east window has five lancets and on the inside of the choir is a sedilia with rounded arches. Within the churches are the recumbent figures on the tombs of the members of the Menteith family now rather weather beaten.

Perhaps the most interesting fact relating to the Priory is that Mary, Queen of Scots and her four Maries were safely housed there after the Battle of Pinkie in 1547, until they could safely be taken to France in the following summer. A lasting memorial to the monks remains in the fine walnut trees, which stand on the lawns surrounding the church, and are believed to have been grown from seeds brought from Rome.

Dunblane Cathedral

Four miles from Stirling on the north bank of the Allan Water is the interesting little town of Dunblane with its magnificent cathedral around which still remain a number of finely restored houses of the seventeenth, eighteenth and even earlier centuries. The cathedral built in pointed Gothic style has been acclaimed the most perfect example of a Scottish medieval church and Ruskin wrote in praise of the splendour of the west front.

It is believed that there was a religous house on the site as early as the 7th century when St. Blane of the Columbian church settled in Dunblane. The diocese was founded by David I in 1150 and it may be that the lower part of the tower belongs to that time. Most of the building dates from the 13th century and careful restorations of the nave in the 19th century and the choir in the twentieth makes Dunblane one of the finest churches in Scotland.

The nave consists of eight bays with aisles, the choir of six without aisles, and there is a north chapel with vaulted roof which runs parallel to the choir but separated by a solid wall. The choir, later than the nave, has fine tall traceried windows but the nave is the finest part of the interior. The clerestory comes down to the top of the arches thus making the aisles low. The clerestory and west windows have an inner and outer wall with a passage running between them. On the inner wall two arches rest on the clustered shafts on each bay and the same sort of construction has been used with good effect on the west window.   All the capitals of the clustered piers are moulded, but the lack of carving gives the whole church an austere dignity.

The west front is the most distinguished part of the exterior and merits the praise of Ruskin. The central doorway is deeply recessed with a series of shafts and mouldings flanked by a sharply pointed blind arch on each side. Above are three very tall pointed windows of equal height, each divided into two lights by a central mullion, the centre arch heads filled with cinquefoil, and the two outside with quatrefoil openings. Above in the gable is an ornamental oval, pointed window.

Six finely carved choir stalls survive from pre-Reformation times but following the restoration were placed at the west end of the church. Near the cathedral is the house of Bishop Leighton where in an upper room reached by an outside stair is housed the library of early books bequethed to the town, following his death in Sussex in 1684. The Bishop, a man of peace resigned his office during the turbulent times when Scotland resented episcopacy. Now parish church of the little town, the cathedral stands at its centre in great dignity and peacefulness.

Dunkeld Cathedral

In the heart of the beautiful Perthshire scenery, lie the remains of Dunkeld Cathedral. Its long history began when the first Celtic church on Iona was destroyed by the Vikings. King Kenneth Macalpine had some of the relics of St. Columba brought to Dunkeld where a monastery was established in 850. For a time it was the metropolitan See of the Celtic church.

Nothing is left of the early monastery but in the reign of Alexander I a group of monks from Scone settled in the area and new abbey buildings were erected, but these too have perished. The earliest parts, belonging to the 13th century are to be seen in the choir and much 15th century work survived the extensive reconstruction undertaken last century. Like Dunblane the abbey has a long narrow choir, no transepts and a nave with aisles. On the north side of the choir is a two-storied chapter-house and a sacristy with groined vaulting. In the nave are the remains of a south porch and there is a tall north-west tower - a later addition and rather English in style.

The ground floor of the tower is vaulted and in it a wall painting of the Judgement of Solomon, one of the finest of its kind in Scotland. The splendid altar tomb of the famous Wolf of Badenock - son of Robert II can be seen in what forms the vestibule of the parish church.

Crosraguel Abbey

On the road from Maybole to Turnberry are the picturesque ruins of Crosraguel Abbey. Founded as an oratory by the Earl of Carrick in 1214, it was later colonised from Paisley as a Clunaic Abbey. It obtained much of its wealth from King Robert the Bruce and his successors, but it suffered great destruction in the Wars of Independence.

The abbey was restored and enlarged at the beginning of the 15th century. The church plan resembles that of the collegiate churches of the period. It is long and narrow without transepts or aisles and has a unique feature in the choir, a three sided apse, one of the earliest in Scotland. The monastic buildings are enclosed by a precinct wall with a massive gate-house, and include a sacristy and chapter-house on the east side, the refectory, parallel to the church on the south. A tiny stream flowing through the beautifully kept grounds adds to the beauty of the abbey setting.

Kilwinning Abbey

In contrast the remains of Kilwinning Abbey present a rather forlorn picture, for the parish church has been built on the choir area and the churchyard covers much of its foundations. Like Kelso, Kilwinning was a Tironesian foundation, dating from the second half of the 12th century but what survives of the building is mostly 13th century. This consists of the tall south transept containing three long pointed arch windows with a circular window in the gable. The chapter-house door is in the same style and there is an exceedingly fine doorway leading from the cloister to the nave. Enough of the west wall remains to indicate a western transept, as at Kelso.

Glenluce Abbey

In the county of Wigtown stands the remains of Glenluce Abbey, founded by Roland, Lord of Galloway, in 1191-2 for monks from Dundrennan. Like so many other abbeys it occupies an attractive site by the riverside, and a unique feature still in its original position is the water supply system with earthenware pipes. Of the church buildings fragments of the south wall, the lower sections of the west front, the south transept, parts of the choir still stand, but, the outstanding attraction is the particularly fine late 15th century chapter-house, which is complete.

It consists of a square apartment below ground level, enclosed by a ribbed vault rising from a central pier. The doorway is round headed with carved decoration and is lit by two wide arched windows with tracery. The floor was laid with glazed tiles, some of which can still be seen.

Whithorn Priory

On the south west peninsula of Wigtownshire tucked away behind the main street in Whithorn and reached through 'the Pends' - a picturesque archway - stand the ruins of the Abbey. The earliest church in the site was one of the first Celtic monasteries in Scotland founded by St. Ninian and dedicated to St. Martin of Tours. It is referred to in the writings of the Venerable Bede. When excavations took place on the site the remains of this tiny white plastered church were discovered below the sanctuary of the 12th century priory church. This was in keeping with the practice of building on holy ground for the shrine of St. Ninian had been a place of pilgrimage for centuries before the founding of the abbey.

Dundrennan Abbey

Dundrennan Abbey, a Cistercian foundation from Rievault, sponsored by David I was begun in 1142 and is typical of the transition period of Cistercian gothic having pointed arches with round headed windows. Excavations of the foundations reveal that the monastery was extensive and the church large, but little remains standing except the west wall with its fine richly decorated doorway and the parts of the transepts. The interior of the transepts show clearly the development of the pointed arch and rib vaulting in Scottish architecture. A new chapter-house erected towards the end of the 13th century is a very fine example of this decorated gothic.

Few places have succeeded in retaining such an air of tranquility as has Dundrennan Abbey, situated in a secluded glen, surrounded by trees, near a stream flowing into the Solway. After the Battle of Langside in 1568, Mary Queen of Scots sought sanctuary at Dundrennan Abbey for her last night in Scotland, before sailing to England to spend the rest of her life in captivity.